D0880853

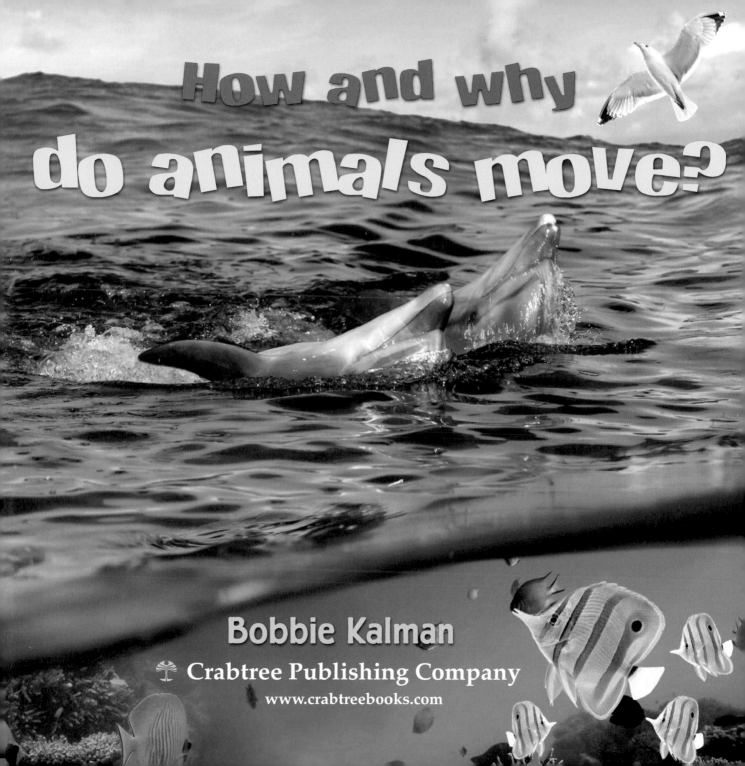

How and why
do animals move?

Bobbie Kalman

Crabtree Publishing Company
www.crabtreebooks.com

For Klaudia Mach
a lovely, intelligent, amazing young woman
in London, England.
Peter and I look forward to meeting you!

Author and editor-in-chief
Bobbie Kalman

Publishing plan research and development
Reagan Miller

Editor
Kathy Middleton

Proofreader
Crystal Sikkens

Photo research
Bobbie Kalman

Design
Bobbie Kalman
Katherine Berti
Samantha Crabtree (cover)

Print and production coordinator
Katherine Berti

Photographs
Thinkstock: page 11 (bottom left)
iStockphoto: page 13 (left)
Other images by Shutterstock

Library and Archives Canada Cataloguing in Publication

Kalman, Bobbie, author
    How and why do animals move? / Bobbie Kalman.

(All about animals close-up)
Includes index.
Issued in print and electronic formats.
ISBN 978-0-7787-0554-3 (bound).--ISBN 978-0-7787-0616-8 (pbk.).--
ISBN 978-1-4271-7594-6 (pdf).--ISBN 978-1-4271-7589-2 (html)

    1. Animal locomotion--Juvenile literature. I. Title.

QP301.K336 2014   j573.7'9   C2014-903911-5
                                           C2014-903912-3

Library of Congress Cataloging-in-Publication Data

Kalman, Bobbie.
 How and why do animals move? / Bobbie Kalman.
    pages. cm -- (All about animals close-up.)
Includes index.
ISBN 978-0-7787-0554-3 (reinforced library binding) -- ISBN 978-0-7787-0616-8
(pbk.) -- ISBN 978-1-4271-7594-6 (electronic pdf) -- ISBN 978-1-4271-7589-2
(electronic html)
 1. Animal locomotion--Juvenile literature. I. Title.

QP301.K279 2015
591.5'7--dc23
                                           2014022881

Crabtree Publishing Company

www.crabtreebooks.com   1-800-387-7650

Printed in the U.S.A./092014/JA20140811

Published in Canada
Crabtree Publishing
616 Welland Ave.
St. Catharines, Ontario
L2M 5V6

Published in the United States
Crabtree Publishing
PMB 59051
350 Fifth Avenue, 59th Floor
New York, New York 10118

Published in the United Kingdom
Crabtree Publishing
Maritime House
Basin Road North, Hove
BN41 1WR

Published in Australia
Crabtree Publishing
3 Charles Street
Coburg North
VIC 3058

Contents

Why do animals move?

Like people, animals are living things. They need air, food, water, and a place to live. Animals move from place to place to get the things they need to survive, or stay alive. They move to find food and **shelter** and to escape from danger. Animals also move to find food and water in new **habitats**. Why and how do people move?

Predators move to find prey, or the animals they hunt and eat. Prey, like this rabbit, move to escape predators.

4

Moving away and back

When seasons change, some animals cannot survive in their habitats. These animals migrate, or move to new habitats for a certain length of time. To learn about animals that migrate, turn to pages 20–21.

Arctic terns migrate farther than any other animal. They fly from the North Pole to the South Pole and back each year. Along the way, they find food in the oceans.

How do they move?

The bodies of animals are built for the way they move. Some animals have wings, some have legs, some have fins or flippers, and some just slide along on their long bodies. Animals that live in water have different body parts that allow them to move in different ways than animals that move on land.

Most birds use their wings to fly (see pages 8–9).

Animals with legs walk, hop, and climb. This lemur is hopping (see page 13).

Snakes slither by twisting their long bodies into curves.

dolphins

penguin

Swimming in oceans

Penguins are birds that cannot fly. Instead, they use their wings to swim in the ocean. Dolphins swim and leap high out of the ocean.

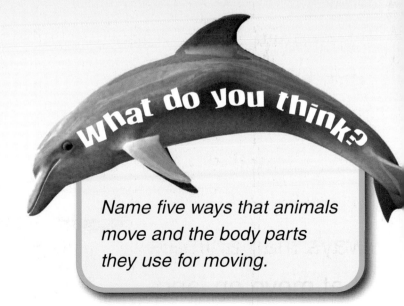

What do you think?

Name five ways that animals move and the body parts they use for moving.

Which animals fly?

flapping ducks

Wings are like arms covered with feathers or flaps of skin. Most animals with wings are able to fly. Birds fly by flapping, or moving their wings up and down. Hummingbirds can hover, or move their wings quickly to stay in one place, while they eat.

hovering hummingbird

Gliding and flapping

Birds can also glide. They keep their wings stretched out and let the air carry them. Bats can fly but not glide. They must keep flapping their wings to stay in the air.

gliding kite

Butterflies flutter, or move their wings very fast while they fly. They can also glide.

flapping bat

fluttering butterflies

What do you think?

Which animal cannot glide? Name two words that mean "flapping quickly."

9

How many legs?

Some animals have two legs, and some have four. There are also animals with many more legs. Some animals with legs can walk, hop, jump, crawl, and run. Some can climb and swim, as well.

Horses can walk, run, swim, and jump. In which ways are they not able to move?

hoofs with one toe

This mother horse and her foal, or baby, run on four legs. Each leg has one toe covered by a hoof, which is made of a hard material. When a horse gallops, or runs very fast, all four legs are off the ground for a short time.

Ducks have two legs with **webbed** feet that act like paddles to help them move in water.

This leopard cub uses its four legs and sharp claws to climb a tree so it can pounce, or jump down, on its prey.

Centipedes crawl on their many legs.

Raccoons are good tree climbers and can hang upside down using their four legs and paws.

What do you think?

Which three animals on these pages can run fast? Why do you think so?

Hop and leap

Most animals with legs can walk and run, but some move by hopping and leaping. Kangaroos, rabbits, frogs, and some lemurs can move quickly when they hop and leap.

Kangaroos use their back legs for hopping. Their thick, long tails help balance their bodies while they hop.

(right) The kangaroo joey, or baby, on the right is learning how to hop. It does not go too far from its mother's pouch, or pocket, where it lives and drinks its mother's milk.

pouch

Long back legs

Animals that hop have long, strong hind, or back, legs. They find it easier to leap than to walk. They can also change direction quickly while they are hopping.

(left) Sifakas are lemurs that live mainly in trees. On the ground, they leap and hop to get around. They look as if they are dancing! (See page 23.)

Hares belong to the rabbit family. Like rabbits, they hop and leap quickly. Their leaps can be as long as 10 feet (three meters) at a time.

Climb, swing, and hang

claws

Some animals live in trees, where they find food and can keep their babies safe from many predators. To climb, animals grip tree trunks with their four legs. Some, such as squirrels, have sharp claws for gripping. Many monkeys and apes swing from tree branch to tree branch using their long arms. A few animals can hang from trees using their **prehensile** tails, which curl around branches.

Orangutans spend most of their time in trees, where they sleep and find food. They use their long arms to swing from tree to tree.

What do you think?

Which other animals in this book can climb trees? Which body parts do they use to help them climb? How do you climb trees?

Some monkeys, like this howler monkey, can hang from trees by their tails. Hanging leaves their paws free to reach for food.

15

High on mountains

Some animals have body parts that help them climb mountains. For example, mountain goats have hoofs. Hoofed animals are able to climb steep rocks to escape most predators—except those that climb mountains, too!

Two-toed hoofs help grip rocks better than hoofs with one toe. They keep mountain goats from sliding as they climb.

Mountain lions

Mountain lions can climb trees using their strong legs and sharp claws. From high up, they can pounce on top of prey. Their large paws also make it easier for them to climb rocks.

What do you think?

How are the hoofs of horses different from those of mountain goats? Name four ways that mountain lions move.

Moving in water

All kinds of animals live in water. The bodies of different animals help them swim in different ways. Most fish move their bodies, fins, and tails to push themselves forward. Some fish, such as sharks, move in a side-to-side motion to keep swimming.

flipper

Dolphins have flippers on their tails. They move them up and down to help them swim.

Why do they leap? Dolphins are **mammals** that need to breathe air above water. They use their flippers to swim fast and to leap out of the water to breathe.

A sea turtle can move both on land and in water. Its flippers work better in water, however, where the turtle flaps them like wings. Which bird swims this way? (See page 7 if you do not know.)

What do you think?

How do these animals swim in different ways? Name four different body parts that help them swim.

Fish, such as this shark, move their bodies from side to side in waves.

An octopus moves in three ways. It can crawl along the ocean floor on its arms or walk slowly on two arms. To move quickly, the octopus takes water into its body and then squirts it out. This powerful squirt moves the octopus backward.

Why do they migrate?

Animals migrate to escape cold weather, find food or water, or have babies. Monarch butterflies migrate when the weather gets cool in autumn. They fly very far, from Canada and the United States to Mexico, where they spend winter.

When the monarchs reach their winter homes, they land on trees and sleep until spring arrives. They then start their trip home.

Finding what they need

Many kinds of birds and whales migrate to warmer places before winter and back home again in spring. Land animals, such as caribou and elephants, migrate to find food when there is not enough to eat where they are.

Canada geese migrate in a V formation. Flying this way keeps them from getting too tired.

Whales that live in cold oceans swim to warm oceans to have their calves, or babies. After the calves have grown bigger, the mothers take them back to the cold oceans, where there is more food to eat.

How do we move?

We have two legs and two arms, but we can swim, climb, and leap, as well as walk and run. We have even learned to fly! People have copied the ways that animals move so that they, too, can move in those ways. Which animals have they copied?

Which animals have flippers for swimming?

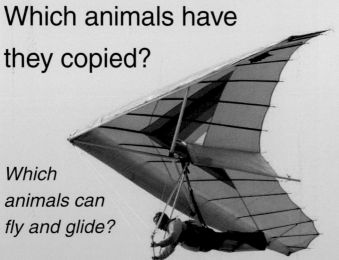

Which animals can fly and glide?

Which animals migrate to warm places for the winter?

Learning more

Books

Kalman, Bobbie. *Animals move like this* (My World).
Crabtree Publishing Company, 2011.

Kalman, Bobbie. *Hip-hop dancers* (My World).
Crabtree Publishing Company, 2010.

Kalman, Bobbie. *Why do animals migrate?* (Big Science Ideas).
Crabtree Publishing Company, 2009.

Koontz, Robin. *Leaps and Creeps: How Animals Move to Survive*
(Amazing Animal Skills). Benchmark Books, 2011.

Websites

Dancing Lemurs of Madagascar
www.youtube.com/watch?v=64FP3bDr8_U

Idaho Public Television: Dialogue for Kids: Animal Migration Facts
http://idahoptv.org/dialogue4kids/season13/animal_migration/facts.cfm

NASA: Animals on the move, Migration Concentration game
http://spaceplace.nasa.gov/migration/en/#

Words to know

habitat (HAB-i-tat) noun The natural area or environment in which a plant or animal lives

mammal (MAM-uh-l) noun A warm-blooded animal that gives birth to live young

predator (PRED-uh-tawr) noun An animal that hunts other animals for food

prehensile (pri-HEN-sil) adjective Describing a body part that is used for grasping objects

prey (prey) noun An animal that is hunted by another animal

shelter (SHEL-ter) noun A place that gives protection from weather or danger

webbed (webd) adjective Describing feet with thin sheets of skin between the toes. Webbed feet act as paddles that help animals swim better and faster through water.

A noun is a person, place, or thing. An adjective is a word that tells you what something is like.

Index